Tell your stories and turn them into a book. It's a great way to witness you and other people who are important to you.

> *From the beginning of the human race stories have been used — by priests, by bards, by medicine men — as magic instruments of healing, of teaching — as a means of helping people come to terms with the fact that they continually have to face insoluble problems and unbearable realities.*
>
> *- Joan Aiken*

If writing is difficult for you, record your thoughts and information on a recorder, iPhone, iPad or smart phone, so you play your thoughts back to yourself because your story matters and you need to listen to it.

Copyright © 2014 Beth Lord

All rights reserved. No part of this book may be reproduced, stored or transmitted by any means without written permission of both publisher and author, except in the case of brief excerpts used in articles and reviews. Unauthorized reproduction of any part of this book is illegal and is punishable by laws. All photographs are the property of Beth Lord.

ISBN: 1622690028
ISBN-13: 978-1-62269-002-2

## DEDICATION

To the pilgrims who walk this way.
It's Your journey.

## ACKNOWLEDGMENTS

To those who made the trip in spirit with me, my sister (Linda), my husband (Grant), and my daughters (Katie, Ame and Samantha).
To Monique who walked it in the Spring and helped my last minute journey preparation.
To Jean Pierre & Josette who offered me a comfortable bed the night before I started on The Camino.

To the pilgrims who walked with me and became my Camino Family:
Lisa, Ele, & Tom,
John, Anne, Declan, Robin, Kevin,
John S., Mark, Prabho, Brian, Lucie, Valle,
Sarah, Mary, Heesu, Wieteke, Olafia,
Pauline, Wayne, Fran, Greg, Elaine, Tanya,
Barbara, Wolfgang, Jacqueline, Claudine, Chris W.,
and everyone else.

# Buen Camino!

## The Minute We Are
## by
## Beth Lord

The minute we are,
we are whole
in our body, mind, heart and soul.

But then we forget
and become pieces of the whole.

If someone listens to our pieces,
we remember,
we have always been whole.

We feel the feelings of these pieces,
we remember,
we have always been whole.

When we walk The Camino de Santiago,
this process happens naturally as we
walk this sacred path.
We move and talk with our fellow pilgrims.
We move and talk within ourselves too.
We walk to remember our wholeness.

The minute we are,
we are whole
in our body, mind, heart and soul.

There are web-sites, books, documentaries and other movies on this subject. This book is for those who have walked The Camino, the curious people who want to take this pilgrimage and for those who cannot walk such a distance but would like to walk it for self-reflection. Here is your book and your journey.

Camino-related resources:

www.santiago-compostela.net

www.theway-themovie.com/camino.php

www.caminodocumentary.org

www.caminoguides.com/guide.html

When I walked The Camino de Santiago, I had many "ah-ha" moments. These "ah-ha" moments or epiphanies were my points of consciousness that connected me to my inner dialogue within myself. I wrote them down as my way markers because I wanted to remember what was going on within me and how I was changing.

So I write this book as my points of consciousness from The Camino to help and encourage you, my fellow pilgrim, in heart and soul to promote your self-awareness.

You ARE whole, and you are amazing because you're you.

What journey are you going on? It can be a physical or inner one. Write what you want to write here. We'll begin our journey together.

The Shell is a symbol of The Camino de Santiago. Pilgrims used it to grab water from the streams and rivers to quench their thirst.

http://caminoways.com/the-scallop-shell-and-the-camino-de-santiago#.VwrL9RMrLm0

What is the symbol that you are taking with you on your journey?

_____

_____

_____

_____

Why?

I'm going on this journey; it's as simple as that. The movement of climbing mountains, carrying my backpack and breathing to get me through this is going to focus my energy, so I'm not distracted. It is easy to get distracted in my "normal" life. I can already tell that it is mighty powerful to have no distractions going on. I have to walk, and this focus step-by-step gives me a greater sense of who I am then when I'm distracted.

**Stop the distraction and focus on what life is showing me.**

What do you need to do my friend?

1._____

_____

_____

2._____

_____

_____

3._____

_____

_____

There is no right nor wrong way to discover who I am. Learning to walk at my pace is a metaphor for this self-discovery, self-healing and self-acceptance process.

It is my choice if I want to grab a notebook & keep track of what I'm learning about myself. It's about noticing me when I'm not distracted.

So I'm giving you equal space to write your journey. This way you don't have to go about finding a notebook because you have one in this book.

**What do you notice?**

No telling what discoveries we're going to find. You can list your findings here and write further about it on the page you write it on. This way, you'll have your content organized.

| Discovery Organizer | Page |
|---|---|
| _____ | _____ |
| _____ | _____ |
| _____ | _____ |
| _____ | _____ |
| _____ | _____ |
| _____ | _____ |
| _____ | _____ |
| _____ | _____ |
| _____ | _____ |
| _____ | _____ |
| _____ | _____ |
| _____ | _____ |
| _____ | _____ |
| _____ | _____ |
| _____ | _____ |

Points of Consciousness from The Camino

## Discovery Organizer Page

| Discovery Organizer | Page |
|---|---|
|  |  |
|  |  |
|  |  |
|  |  |
|  |  |
|  |  |
|  |  |
|  |  |
|  |  |
|  |  |
|  |  |
|  |  |
|  |  |
|  |  |
|  |  |
|  |  |
|  |  |
|  |  |
|  |  |

Points of Consciousness from The Camino

What are my top 10 needs that can be prioritized and rearranged as I go along on this way?

1._____

2._____

3._____

4._____

5._____

6._____

7._____

8._____

9._____

10._____

Here's a few more if you need them.

11. _____

12._____

13._____

14._____

15._____

When I care for my basic needs it's easier for me to feel burdens I don't need to carry.

Baggage is another term for burden. So it's time to find that rock that represents a burden I want to let go of at Cruz de Ferro (Iron Cross) which is the highest point on The French Camino

http://letallwhoarethirstycome.blogspot.com/2014/08/camino-de-santiago-cruz-de-ferro.html

http://www.galiciaguide.com/Stage-25.html

Why don't you find a rock, pebble or stone that represents your burden? I think it is perfectly okay to gather up as many stones as you want providing you know what burden that stone represents to you. You may keep this information private and confidential, tell people about these burdens or write them down.

My Burden Of Rocks

1. Rock     Burden _____

2. Rock     Burden_____

3. Rock     Burden _____

4. Rock     Burden_____

5. Rock     Burden _____

I have a backpack for my basic needs and walking sticks to help me along. If you aren't taking the physical journey then what are you taking along to help you with your journey. This can be something real or it can be a thought, a prayer, a picture.

_____

_____

_____

We open the door to the unknown.

This journey has ancient ruins, beautiful scenery, and camaraderie so I am awake and paying attention. Even though the languages and words may be different, everyone has a focus on moving and getting to the next point. I find the rhythm and pace I need to move me forward. The fewer burdens I have to carry, the easier it is for me to go into myself. This walking focus is something that's practical and mystical, so both the individual and the group feels supported.

I am a pilgrim on The Camino. I breathe to remember this.

Walking with this backpack on intensifies the awareness of me and my movement. I suppose that's why I notice my breath, my heart beating, my arms and hands, my legs and feet. So if I'm not walking can I notice me working as one unit to get me from Point A to Point B?

Yes   or   No?

My thoughts on my backpack:

_____

_____

_____

_____

_____

_____

Life is simple when I am participating in life by moving me along in it. It takes everything I have to get me from Point A to Point B. This is stupendous.

Why don't I give myself credit for being alive?
Yay for being alive.
Hip Hip Hooray!
Hip Hip Hooray!
Hip Hip Hooray!

I think you need to give yourself 3 cheers for being alive too.

★ Hip Hip Hooray!
★ Hip Hip Hooray!
★ Hip Hip Hooray!


I can pick any movement in my body to notice and notice how amazing my bones, joints, nerves, and muscles help propel me forward.

My parts support the whole of me, but my mind doesn't buy the simplicity of how this works and interferes with appreciating me.

Anytime you can tell your mind to "shut up!"

Animals seem to get this.
They know when to move.
They know when to take a break.
They know the speed in which to move.

## Your Animals On This Journey

**Let's Talk About The Dragons We Need To Slay**
What dragons do you need to slay?

_____

_____

_____

_____

_____

_____

_____

If I meet my dragons, I have the power to move them out of my way. I have the power to see if they are helping me or hurting me. Do some dragons want to protect the wholeness of my holiness?

_____

_____

_____

_____

_____

_____

_____

_____

_____

_____

_____

And, by the way, didn't I give these dragons power in the first place?

Listening to peoples' stories are powerful. I learn from them, and this shifts me and my dragons. What stories have moved me that I've heard from my fellow pilgrims?

Story One

_____

_____

_____

_____

_____

Story Two

_____

_____

_____

_____

_____

Story Three




Story Four




Story Five

Points of Consciousness from The Camino

Story Five

_____

_____

_____

Story Six

_____

_____

_____

_____

_____

Story Seven

_____

_____

_____

_____

_____

Story Eight




Story Nine




Story Ten

Story Ten

Story Eleven

Story Twelve

## Story Thirteen

## Story Fourteen

I don't need to know the details of your life if you don't want to share them. If I am myself, I'll give you what you need. I know I have something to share with you and you have something to share with me. But it doesn't have to be details. Maybe, it's a quiet walk. Maybe, it's a smile. Maybe, it's a friendship that develops beyond The Camino.

I help other people who are on this journey because it's natural. Compassion and care is natural on this Camino. Everyone is valued on The Camino. There is no hierarchy. Everyone is a pilgrim.

**Pilgrims I know.**

Name Email Phone

_____

City & Country_____

Details _____
— — — — — — — — — — — — — — — — — — — — —
Name Email Phone

_____

City & Country_____

Details _____

**Pilgrims I know.**

Name                    Email                       Phone
_____

City & Country _____

Details _____

- - - - - - - - - - - - - - - - - - - - - - - -

Name                    Email                       Phone
_____

City & Country _____

Details _____

- - - - - - - - - - - - - - - - - - - - - - - -

Name                    Email                       Phone
_____

City & Country _____

Details _____

- - - - - - - - - - - - - - - - - - - - - - - -

Name                    Email                       Phone
_____

City & Country _____

Details _____

**Pilgrims I know.**

Name                    Email                   Phone

_____

City & Country _____

Details _____
- - - - - - - - - - - - - - - - - - - - - - -
Name                    Email                   Phone

_____

City & Country _____

Details _____
- - - - - - - - - - - - - - - - - - - - - - -
Name                    Email                   Phone

_____

City & Country _____

Details _____
- - - - - - - - - - - - - - - - - - - - - - -
Name                    Email                   Phone

_____

City & Country _____

Details _____

Pilgrims I know.

Name                    Email                    Phone
_____

City & Country _____

Details _____
- - - - - - - - - - - - - - - - - - - - - - - -
Name                    Email                    Phone
_____

City & Country _____

Details _____
- - - - - - - - - - - - - - - - - - - - - - - -
Name                    Email                    Phone
_____

City & Country _____

Details _____
- - - - - - - - - - - - - - - - - - - - - - - -
Name                    Email                    Phone
_____

City & Country _____

Details _____

Pilgrims I know.

| Name | Email | Phone |
|---|---|---|

City & Country _____

Details _____

- - - - - - - - - - - - - - - - - - - -

| Name | Email | Phone |
|---|---|---|

City & Country _____

Details _____

- - - - - - - - - - - - - - - - - - - -

| Name | Email | Phone |
|---|---|---|

City & Country _____

Details _____

- - - - - - - - - - - - - - - - - - - -

| Name | Email | Phone |
|---|---|---|

City & Country _____

Details _____

Pilgrims I know.

| Name | Email | Phone |
|---|---|---|
| | | |

City & Country _____

Details _____

---

| Name | Email | Phone |
|---|---|---|
| | | |

City & Country _____

Details _____

---

| Name | Email | Phone |
|---|---|---|
| | | |

City & Country _____

Details _____

---

| Name | Email | Phone |
|---|---|---|
| | | |

City & Country _____

Details _____

I am getting to know me and what seems to be true. This knowing of me feels courageous. I am courageous! I'm courageous, and I didn't realize it. Yay for me.

This journey is made up of any narrative I want as long as it gets to the heart of me. Getting to the heart of me is what I'm doing for the rest of my lifetime. That means I'll be going through transitions and transformations to realize myself. I am walking and learning that as I focus, the busy chatter in my mind calms down. And the butterflies in my stomach relax.

If I breathe and relax, I can bring me together in wholeness; accepting the opposing viewpoints within myself. It's okay. My walking sticks provide the ways and the means of giving me support with the inclines and the declines. I don't have to do it alone.

Like the snail, shifting his weight from side to side so he can carry his weight and get to where he's going, that's what I do. Steady movement helps me with life at the moment.

Divine Intervention also crosses my path if I look up and notice that he/she wants to walk with me. This journey is awe-inspiring because it's practical and mysterious. This divine intervention is my link to personal power and the great beyond. It requires nothing but openness.

Divine intervention is sparks of consciousness that come from us igniting with this consciousness in us. So I am a divine spark, and you are a divine spark, and we flame into inspiration, motivation, and responsiveness when we connect within ourselves and with each other.

If I am hungry, I eat. If I am tired, I sleep or take a break. When I wake up, I make choices in how I walk on The Camino. I have only two options when it comes to being a divine spark. I either close down in fear or open up in love.

Why don't you talk it over with someone or write a note to yourself? Better yet, go for a walk and meet up with some Pilgrims. The mystical part of all of this is when I am honest in feeling my feelings and feel them. That's all I was supposed to do was feel my feelings and let them go. My feelings don't have to become burdens I carry around with me.

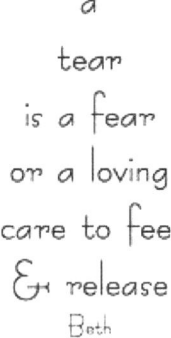

When I remove my fear of getting somewhere, then I am here where I'm supposed to be. If I shift the focus from my mind to the heart NOW, I can feel my brave heart.

Carrying around burdens from my sex, culture & upbringing leaves absolutely no space for me. So maybe I can leave these troubles behind? Because what I am beginning to feel is that I can trust my storyline as I lose the burdens of disbelief in myself.

I make a list of useful and not so useful habits to see which ones are no longer necessary to me so I can think about letting them go.

| Useful Habits | Not-So-Useful Habits |
| --- | --- |
| _____ | _____ |
| _____ | _____ |
| _____ | _____ |
| _____ | _____ |
| _____ | _____ |
| _____ | _____ |
| _____ | _____ |
| _____ | _____ |
| _____ | _____ |
| _____ | _____ |
| _____ | _____ |

Burdens become heavy if I don't pay attention to why I'm talking about them. Is it to solve a problem? Is it to gain attention? Is it to cope? If I listen to myself, I hear the answer.

Time bends around the corner of space and results in feeling like I'm one with the environment. I don't know how this works; I just have to accept that I've been made whole even beyond my comprehension.

Every day I do a little something that devotes time in the search and rescue of me.

# The Everyday Search & Rescue Of Me

## This can include what I find inspiring and motivating.

There's a giving and a receiving on this journey that makes me feel necessary. And the steps I am stepping are my way markers for finding my points of consciousness. These steps I take are one moment at a time. This is how I get to me I've been searching for all along. And let's just say that I'm a doubting Thomas sometimes. That's okay. If I am stepping one step at a time, then I am getting the information that life is change in motion, a fluid ebb, and flow of the moment. I get stuck when I think life is something other than right here and now.

The light I am walking in fills me with energy. And when I go to sleep I feel a mysterious healing going on in my cells giving me energy and health for tomorrow. Compassion grows in me because I am learning to be compassionate within myself. I reach out to others when they need help.

I have a great life. If I don't have a great life, I can edit out the n, the apostrophe, the t and the problem's solved. I can edit and change my life anytime. I breathe love and acceptance into me. Even the things I don't like about me can be loved. My spirit takes every exhale and transforms it into a life-enhancing inhale that nourishes my body, heart, mind and soul. So I keep moving to know the rhythm of me in my breathing, walking, and movement. I am learning lessons I was too busy to notice before I took this journey. The funny thing is that when I stop the busyness and give myself a chance to focus, I feel great.

Listening to the cowbells on cows roaming the countryside is soothing for me to hear. What other sounds soothe the savage beast in me?

_____

_____

_____

_____

_____

_____

_____

_____

_____

Drinking water quenches my thirst, and it's marvelous to taste. I knew I was going to make it up this mountain as long as I took it at my pace and didn't follow the crowd because I know that my determination is fighting immense! I won't apologize for having a turtle's pace with a pack on my back. It's my pace.

What is your pace?

_____

_____

_____

_____

Frequently eating healthy snacks gives me energy and keeps me healthy. I know I'm eating in loving gratitude because it's giving me the energy I need to continue.

I rest. I get to sit in a chair, and I'm amused because it's such a novel way to rest from my normal plopping down on a bench or the ground. I decide to let go of another burden. It's amazing how my backpack is getting lighter.

I walk down the mountain in a downpour. Day hikers offer to drive me to the Albergue. I take them up on their offer, and I know it's a miracle.

Why do I need to have the pain to have these breakthroughs in consciousness? I curse the Holy when it's only myself that needs to take a break from my dangerous actions. I'm at my wit's end so I ask for help, and I receive it. Support comes in an easy and kind, comfortable way. Did I get help because I asked for it?

Hmm, I think this is vital information here. I need to ask for it. I need to know how I'm feeling and reach out. Sometimes, people may be able to guess what's going on but I have to be willing to ask for something. I can be vulnerable.

I walk. I slow down. I shift the weight I'm carrying on my back. I never knew how much panic lived inside of me. My thoughts said they'd protect me from my panic. They did, at the cost of cutting me off from my heart. Cutting me off from my heart to appease my mind is not a good trade-off!

My pain is excruciating. Does anyone feel my pain or is it so subjective that the pain I feel is just between me, myself and I? What's your pain like?

_____

_____

_____

_____

When I put my feet in the river, my feet get relief, and so do I. What other things can I do to soothe and comfort me?

_____

_____

_____

_____

_____

_____

It's nonsense for me to be thinking that my status in life keeps me from my human vulnerability. I am vulnerable like you. But here's the secret, I come with a spark that's divine and so do you. This spark is consciousness, and it's possible for everyone. I push on through my fear. I push on through my pain.

Where's a sanctuary when you need one?

---

I can find a sanctuary to go to or go to the one that's always available on the inside of me.

My nose is to the grindstone, so I don't stumble, and I can get from point A to point B, but I also look up and take in the total view. Wow. It's a beautiful vista, and I take it in. It's lovely to see what's around me. I'm making life simpler by getting rid of the unnecessary. I retract my statement that the pain isn't worth the gain because it must be, I'm still on this journey. This Camino might-as-well-be called moving through my feelings because I recognize I cannot hold on to my emotions. They are as changeable as my feet moving me step-by-step.

I also suspend my habits to see what is necessary for me to be on this journey. Eventually, I'm letting go of the unnecessary habits.

I am grateful for toilet paper. It's easier to wipe my crap away. And what I'm learning is that if I listen to myself, I get a very clear answer.

 I am changing.  How am I changing?

I see butterflies that are free. I think this is a sign for my butterflies to leave my stomach whenever they want to.

Out of nowhere my friend appears, and I wonder how she knew, I needed her? This camaraderie is natural. I share what I have with others, and others share with me. My passport is full. It's stamped with all the places I have gone. But what stamps do I have on my inner passport?

I sob many times throughout this Camino. It must help the airing out of my soul. My butterflies have transformed and are no longer in my stomach. I feel I have been changed too because my suffering is gone and I feel joy. I know I am taken care of on this journey. What was my fear? I like being with me and I like being with people. I feel on this Camino that something far greater than myself works with life. I can depend on this. I let go of nervousness. I relax and see what's going to help as I live my life. I laugh because laughter opens up my heart and soul.

I know that I can take my rocks back home. But then they're like pets needing to be fed and taken care of so the rocks go. It makes a great difference in my posture and gait. The rhythm of me pushing on and letting go is giving me a new perspective on life.

How are you and your rocks?

_____

_____

_____

_____

_____

I meet people, and they talk. I listen carefully to them because I know they have a message for me. When I speak, I know I have a message for that person, but I don't worry what part of the conversation holds the key for them because they'll know.

I am so much more than I thought I was. This awareness is remarkable for me to feel in myself. I breathe and feel from my heart. If I forget and let my mind take over, it takes me back to what it knows, and that is fear. However, I keep it focused on both my logic and intuition working together to give me the answers I need.

I walk in the rain and mind the puddles for my neighbor and me. I speak up when I see, hear and feel something isn't right. I have no time for self-indulgence. It's a burden I left behind. It's very different than self-care, self-acceptance, and love for who I am. I give to life as the water coming out of the fountain in a steady state of expression. As I finish this journey, I know what I'm taking back home is the momentum I naturally learned in giving and receiving on this Camino.

I let go of competing with other people by trying to keep up with everyone else who was passing me. I work at my pace. I have learned that sometimes, it is best to be silent and listen. I know I wrap around society's acceptance, but I got to know the skin I'm wearing in this game and that's what I've done by going on The Camino.

I can take care of my discomfort now.
I sleep.
I relax.
I focus and meditate.
I trust the indivisible process in me.
I break down the barriers that hold me back from trusting life.
I say both Yes and No in the revolving door of my holiness that lives within me. It's up to me to make sure I'm warm and comfortable or cool and comfortable. I don't have to apologize for being me as long as I'm being me. Let time, place and the burden go.

Let love remove the residue and the wind blow it away.

**Buen Camino!**

Beth Lord

## My Story

## My Story

## My Story

## My Story

Beth Lord

## My Story

www.ingramcontent.com/pod-product-compliance
Lightning Source LLC
LaVergne TN
LVHW010019070426
835507LV00001B/8